Jeremy Keeps His Promise

Viola Lee Ann
Webb-Williams

TEACH Services, Inc.
PUBLISHING
www.TEACHServices.com • (800) 367-1844

Copyright © 2019 Viola Lee Ann Webb-Williams

Copyright © 2019 TEACH Services, Inc.

ISBN-13: 978-1-4796-1150-8 (Paperback)

ISBN-13: 978-1-4796-1151-5 (ePub)

Library of Congress Control Number: 2019920288

TEACH Services, Inc.
P U B L I S H I N G
www.TEACHServices.com • (800) 367-1844

Dedication

To all Young Jeremy's family, godparents, and friends—

Kevin, Antione, Joshua, La Netta, Claude, Vaneice, and Latoya, and to all of Jeremy's other friends who grew up to introduce the love of Jesus to their children personally.

I also dedicate this book to Neorah (7) and Nyla (6), my great-nieces who gave their personal approval to this children's book.

"Therefore I say to you, whatever things you ask when you pray, believe that you receive *them,* and you will have *them*" (Mark 11:24, NKJV).

Acknowledgements

A special thank you to Jondra (MiMi) Grier for her beautiful artwork and a special praise to God for providing His assigned publishing company to get this book published.

Thanks to Ruth Barkley, who supported me every step of the way to the completion of this children's book.

I thank God for my four relentless "faith" prayer partners—Cheryl Jones-Woodward-Bennett, Gladys Richardson, Richard Cooper, and Irvin Sutton—and for my family and friends who believed in my faith relationship with God our Heavenly Father, Jesus Christ our Savior, and the Holy Spirit living in many of us.

Jeremy burst into the room yelling excitedly, "Mama, Mama! Kevin's dog had puppies! Can I have one? I *promise* I will take care of him! I'll take care of him all by myself!"

Mama said, "I don't think you are old enough to take care of a small puppy Jeremy—you are only seven years old."

"I'm almost eight! I promise I can take care of him Mama! Please! Please!"

Mama replied, "I'll talk to your dad when he comes home from work, Jeremy, and hear what he thinks about this idea of getting a puppy."

Jeremy burst into the room yelling excitedly, "Mama, Mama! Kevin's dog had puppies! Can I have one? I *promise* I will take care of him! I'll take care of him all by myself!"

Mama said, "I don't think you are old enough to take care of a small puppy Jeremy—you are only seven years old."

"I'm almost eight! I promise I can take care of him Mama! Please! Please!"

Mama replied, "I'll talk to your dad when he comes home from work, Jeremy, and hear what he thinks about this idea of getting a puppy."

Smiling, Dad replied, "Give me time to talk to your mom, son," as he picked up Jeremy and gave him a big hello hug.

Dad went inside and talked with Mom. After a few minutes they decided to let Jeremy have a puppy.

Dad said, "Okay, Jeremy, we will let you have a puppy, but you will have to feed and love your puppy or Mama and I will give him to someone who will."

Jeremy sat on the steps all evening waiting on Dad to come home.

Finally, Jeremy saw Dad's car pulling into the driveway.

"Dad! Dad!" cried Jeremy, "Kevin's dog has puppies and Mama wants to tell you I want one! Can I have one? Can I? Can I Dad?"

www.ingramcontent.com/pod-product-compliance
Lightning Source LLC
Chambersburg PA
CBHW061407090426

42739CB00022B/3501

Little Spud grew up to be a big, healthy, and happy dog.

Mama and Dad were very proud of how well Jeremy cared for Spud and most of all, how well he kept his promises.

Sun, rain, or snow, Jeremy fed, watered, and played with his little puppy.

One snowy day, it was so cold that Jeremy wanted to just stay inside where it was nice and warm. But did this stop him from caring for his puppy?

Not at all! After putting on his hat, coat, and snow boots, Jeremy made a path to Spud's dog house to feed and walk Spud.

Mama and Dad took Jeremy to Kevin's house to look at the puppies.

"Oh boy!! I want that one with the patch over his eye! I'll call him Spud. And I *promise* to take really good care of him!"